TWINKLE, TWINKLE, SOCIAL MEDIA STAR

AN INTERNET FAIRYTALE OF FAME, FORTUNE & FOLLOWERS

KATE KENNEDY

Illustrated by TORIE CONN

Ulysses Press

Published in the United States by:
Ulysses Press
P.O. Box 3440
Berkeley, CA 94703
www.ulyssespress.com

ISBN: 978-1-61243-830-6
Library of Congress Catalog Number: 2018955524

Printed in the United States by Bang Printing
10 9 8 7 6 5 4 3 2 1

Acquisitions: Casie Vogel
Managing editor: Claire Chun
Editor: Claire Sielaff
Proofreader: Shayna Keyles
Front cover design: Ashley Prine

Distributed by Publishers Group West

To my parents, Colleen and Jim:
For always making me feel like a star.

Darling, when you grow up, I hope
You will be whatever you want.
As long as you're not a doctor,
Lawyer, or some sort of savant.

Not a teacher, chef, nor farmer...
My love, these just won't do!
Look out there even farther,
Past the sun, the sky, the moon!

Darling, please know, I understand
You will be whoever you are,
But why shoot for the moon, when you could land
Among social media stars?

Some people say, "Do what you love,"
I say, "Do what gets you likes!"
Don't just follow dreams, my dear,
Dream of followers at night!

Sweet child, I'll get you some views,
No need to find a scandal,
'Cause while you were in the womb,
I registered your handles.

And to reveal that "it's a girl!"
I said to your dad, we've gotta
Do a live stream, the world must see
Us swinging at a piñata!

And when I went into labor,
Daddy Snapped your whole delivery.
Vine may be dead, but honey,
It's safe to say, not chivalry!

Social media has changed the world,
Our children must be front and center.
We used to keep up with the Joneses
But now we keep up with Kris Jenner.

So dear, these tales will teach you
How to be your online best:
How to post, like, and low-key brag
Under the guise of being #blessed!

Once upon a timeline, you'll find a place
People hope and pray for traffic.
Where an Apple's not a forbidden fruit,
And going viral is pure magic.

This place is called the internet,
And you may find this surprising,
Thanks to your phone, you can be alone,
But still be socializing!

But first you must appear, my dear,
To be happy and healthy,
To be yourself, above all else,
And to believe in your selfie!

And I pray that you won't forget,
While posting OOTDs,
They say you're never fully dressed
Without a smile emoji!

And if that smile fades, the way
To get support when days are long,
Is to post vague status updates
'Til someone asks you what is wrong.

Those near and dear are important, love,
They will be there 'til the end.
But some days call for prayer hands
From a random high school friend.

On a slow day, head to the café
If starving for likes and comments.
Latte art in your oversized mug?
Darling, THAT's what I call content.

Want to run a 5k? Dog needs a spay?
Honey, don't you force it.
Your social network has the money
If you just crowdsource it.

If you haven't left your couch for days,
And are in need of double taps,
Find a time you did something cool,
And then hashtag TAKE ME BACK!

And if you get hungry, don't start chewing
Before you get to snappin',
'Cause if you go to brunch and no one posts it,
Then baby, did it happen?

When a post is only kind of funny,
Don't let honesty get to your head.
Respond not with a mere LOL,
But with tombstone, RIP, DEAD!

And if you fall and are embarrassed,
Simply get back up and kill it!
And if you're extremely lucky, dear,
Just hope that someone filmed it.

Why be mortified when you can monetize?
Baby, start counting those views!
You know what they say, the ole cliché,
The best revenge is ad revenue.

When you need those hits, try clickbait lists.
Write headlines that gently coerce,
Like, "25 things you won't believe
If #23 doesn't kill you first!"

G FALLS OFF WALL KING'S
MPTY BACK TOGETHER AGAIN!!

While others say less is more,
Darling, I say do the most,
Until you have enough followers
To start getting sponsored posts!

A career, my dear, is such old news.
Let your peers get themselves in a tizzy.
Success is less what you do these days,
It's about appearing hashtag busy.

They may tell you that it's not a job,
But they'll eat their words, honey.
You'll be too busy spending all of
That F-U tummy tea money.

Hold your head high, and don't listen
To any of those snobby actresses.
One day they'll lay their head down, wishin'
They could sell memory foam mattresses.

21

Whether it's diet shakes or powders, babe,
Get paid to get rid of those toxins.
The hustle is real, and harder to quit
Than those meal subscription boxes.

But you can inspire while you sell, my belle!
You can't help if they all want to buy it,
Just get their email, and 5 friends as well,
Then 5 of their friends' friends to try it!

But it's not all about looks, sweetie
Make them aspire while you promote!
So mix it up with photos in a bikini,
And hashtag BOSSBABE quotes.

And dear lord, never airbrush a photo
Near a door or backdrop staircase!
Those lines will wiggle even more than you did
Before Photoshopping your waist.

And I don't care who you love, my love,
Or who you bring home one day,
Whether it's a hashtag WCW
Or a man crush Monday.

Just make sure it's the right person for you,

That you've found the mate to your soul.

Do you love, trust, and honor? Sure!

But more importantly, is it #goals?

And I believe in fighting for causes,
All opinions, you must promote!
For without your baseless input,
How will your friends know how to vote?

But if one day you speak too soon,
Don't pout if you can't take it back.
Fear not darling, for it wasn't you!
Just tweet out that you have been hacked!

Today's your day! The world (wide web)'s a stage!
If you will grace it in this role,
Oh, my sweet girl, can you imagine
All of the places you will scroll?

Darling, you will do great things in life,
A best seller! A Pulitzer Prize!
Or even better, a blue check mark
To tell the whole world you're verified.

And if all else fails, never forget
Your following will grow much faster
If you can become a self-produced
TV villain on The Bachelor.

But I hope you know this is all for fun.
While we love to like, follow, and tweet,
There's more to life than likes to be won:
Look up at the sky, not your screen.

My love, my cub, when all's said and done,
Your best days aren't on a profile page.
Forget your accounts, it's what's on the inside that counts.
The best impressions to make are not paid.

So Twinkle, Twinkle, my little star
While internet fame is not too far,
No matter what, you'll shine so bright,
Like an iPhone screen late at night.

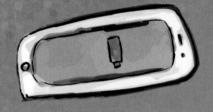

Twinkle, Twinkle, Social Media Star,
There's so much more to who you are.

About the Author

© Bayly Shelley

KATE KENNEDY is a Chicago-based entrepreneur who is best known for her brand Be There in Five. After her signature product, the "remindoormat," took off unexpectedly, Kate had to leave her corporate marketing job to run her hobby-turned-business full-time. After starting a business and facing the necessary perils of social media self-promotion, Kate was inspired to write this book, which pairs her love for rhyming with commentary about today's influencer economy from an outsider's point of view. Kate and her products have been featured in *Glamour, Self, Martha Stewart Living, RealSimple, Teen Vogue, Huffington Post*, BuzzFeed, Refinery29, and more. Her love for social media comes from experience; she can be found on Instagram (@bethereinfive), bethereinfive.com, and via her podcast, Be There in Five.

About the Illustrator

TORIE CONN is an illustrator who was born and raised in the city of Chicago. She received a bachelor of fine arts degree from Denison University in Granville, Ohio. She also studied at School of the Art Institute of Chicago and Pratt Institute in Brooklyn, New York. Torie's current work ranges from small-format ink and watercolor pieces to large-scale public art inspired by the simple joys and ironies of daily life.